Three More Days

AAKASH TYAGI

Copyright © 2018 Aakash Tyagi

All rights reserved.

ISBN: 0692095810
ISBN-13: 978-0692095812

this book is yours now.

"You begin saving the world by saving one man at a time; all else is grandiose romanticism or politics."

- Charles Bukowski

ACKNOWLEDGMENTS

This book is presented as a work of fiction. It has been in existence for a while now, full of stories about the people I have known. But few of them played a bigger role in ruining my nights in order to finish this book, so this is me dedicating this space to them.

Lizzy, Sushi, Sameep, Cristian, Dr. Narain, Nikki, Raavi, y'all are great at giving feedback. Well, most of you.

Ellen, thanks for editing and the conclusion, and teaching me about prepositions.

Meg, thanks for reading my mind and painting it on the cover.

The 23 people who read my blog, y'all are the real MVP.

Mum and dad, *waves*.

And everyone else, hit me up. Let's get coffee.

INTRODUCTION

Around five years ago, I met this guy. He told me he's got a wonderful story for me to write. One to which I can't say no. Something so real that it will find its breath in the reader's eyes and will live on forever in their mundane existence.

Bullshit, I said.

"No seriously, you have to trust me on this. I know my shit. Better than you or anyone else does."

There was a pause. He lit up his cigarette and smoked the warmth away, being the caretaker of a cold southern day.

"I've lived better than you can ever dream of."

This guy was adamant. His eyes weren't lying. He looked massively hungover. You could taste the vomitus of the night before from his breath, even though he had tried his best to wash himself down the drain holes of 7/11. He then took a hit of his leftover number seven.

And what have you ever done so worthwhile, I asked.

He looked at me, with a curiosity you have when you're starting something new, and put his arm holding the Jack on my right shoulder. He then pulled out a piece of paper from his left pocket and slid it carefully inside my right.

"I'll see you around."

He grinned, and left.

Liar. I never saw him after that. Sometimes I wonder if this book would have been any different if I ever read that piece of paper instead of dumping it in with my empty pack of cigarettes. I like to tell myself that I know, or that I'm fairly certain of what I'd have found on it. But I never really want to know.

Satisfaction is the death of desire.

Instead, I've got this story for you. This story is a usual story. A story about a guy and a girl. They could be anyone. Look around you. To your left. To your right. Look in the mirror. Stare right into those eyes. They could be you too. Maybe it is you. And her.

They could be anyone, and no one. And that's what's so beautiful about them. They could pretend like they were the only two people that God ever intended to create, and they could also pass each other on an empty street and not even care to notice. Even though their bodies knew the other was just a breath away.

>They were intense, yet hollow.

>They were fire, trapped in a snowstorm.

>Burning up to their desires, arctic to their souls.

>Honestly, they were both full of shit.

That's who I think they are. And every other guy and girl who think they are the perfect snowflake descending from Jesus's trench coat on a crisp Christmas eve.

THREE MORE DAYS

Sure, why not?

And I'm Brad Pitt.

Heidi

i took off my glasses to the
sultry moans
to the lights red
as wine.

she took a deep breath
under my ear
guided my hands
to my prize for the night
and told me with her hazel eyes

Love, let me make you alright.

sure as hell
she wasn't lying
she became the moment
and that moment was mine.

Say my name

and all i could say was a smile.
dammit, i blew it again
let's just call you Heidi
for this little while.

chaos

if i stood back
far enough

f   a   r
enough
from the
c

      h

 a

   o

     s

would that
make it

an order?

THREE MORE DAYS

who are you?

i stayed up all night
reading your poetry.

the french brew
and the old and
faithful few
gathered together in the sky
to mystify your
existence
your every breath.

five cups down
and my eyes drown
in a sea of senseless
fear, and lies
and unexplored vices.

i stayed up all night
reading your poetry.

and i still have no clue
what you look like.

moving on

the fresh smell of a newly
laid mattress
on a perfectly assembled
bed frame roars in
the air.

filling the room
with the virtuosity of what
only money can buy.

a quick glimpse
catches the painted reflection
of a newly furnished life.

it's all you've always
wanted to be.

silence.

utter silence.

and then you hear
a water drop traveling
down, reaching for the sink.
to be in touch with
something it
belongs to.

or maybe
your heart wants it
to be that way.

THREE MORE DAYS

this is what
loneliness
looks like.

amaretto sour

i give in
my ears are pink
into thin air
my heart does sink.

from your cranberry lips
cherry juice drips down
slowly, like amaretto
waiting to drown

in the red
of my skin
in the eleventh hour
of my sins.

THREE MORE DAYS

how to write poetry?

you ask
how do I write poetry?

those words that
breathe together in an
unusual way that
stay, with you
and the ones getting wet
in their rain.

there is no secret, darling.

these words
and their jazz that
you claim to hear
are not even real.

the only poetry
I ever saw was in
your hair, hypnotizing
its audience in the
wild wind amphitheater
and in your eyes

when you look
at me, and

smile.

shut up

stop talking.

just show
me your
eyes

and
let me

read.

THREE MORE DAYS

the night before

I love you.

she said, and started walking
down the stairs.
her hair swayed like
Boston leaves.
she stopped outside her car.
her lips
paired with her shrilling green eyes
smiled.

all of that said it all,
Almost all
that's ever been said about love.

she stayed there, waiting
to hear a reply.
one she heard every day.

but this time
my lips didn't move
the way they were accustomed to.
my senses left me and I just stood
gazing into the vastness
of the night before.

there She was
sitting next to me, our legs intertwined
with a little jazz, a bottle of red wine.

with my arm around Her
we reminisced about Our past
for hours
before I lost my way into Her deep blue eyes,
I pulled Her closer
and we closed Our eyes.

soon enough, we both were oxygen
and we were both dying to breathe.

she was still standing
looking at me, her green eyes waiting.
I took in a deep breath
and without a word

went in.

THREE MORE DAYS

longings

a fine printed portrait
of fab four
stares down
at the wrinkled, exclusive
blue canvas
of my bed.

"i need a woman"

one of my pillows
whispers
to the rest.

even the bedside lamp
longs for the
flavor of your blinding hair
and aftertaste
of your
morning smile

every once
in a while.

floored

it wasn't the first time
i got lost in her hair
but the wind paused
and the sky looked over
that time.

looked over me to see
if i was doing fine
and i told him
i didn't even hear him
walking through the door
i never felt him
put his breath down
on my silhouetted floor.

and no it's not that
i don't love him as much
as i did before
only my
existence was clouded by
her hair and i couldn't help
but want more.

THREE MORE DAYS

black + white

i drew some
black and white sketches
last night.

sketches of coffee cups
and steamy words
with no sugar
and cream.

sketches of a bearded moon
hanging with
falling fireflies
and coughing out toxic breaths.

sketches of smoke
and spirits
masking the true sound
of art.

sketches of a lady in
red, walking away
in the rain
under her cover

walking away
from the black and white
sounds, of despair
and pain

of a broken heart

isn't being alone
together
better than
being apart?

perspective

this world is nothing
but a poem
-- poetry without stop --
a hymn, ode and epic
poetry
still flowing.
Apollo and Muses
chanting still.

will these two
separate themselves
from me ever again?

I fear it not.

I'm as real as the things
I see.

coffee

"What do you want?"

i wondered, as i looked
right at the question.

i thought of many things
they never put on the menu.

a job, an old beat-up truck
food, always more food
a little gas, an expensive Strat,
open roads, no speed limits.

freedom.

time.

"By the way, I like your hair."

i'd rather take coffee than
compliments right now.

"And how would you like it?"

black – like my soul.

THREE MORE DAYS

eternity

sip slowly on the
grainy bay, lean back
and look at the
infinite sky.
near the horizon boast
of marking the end
and how the sun stretches it
to eternity.

then smile, knowing
that eternity is

at the bottom of your glass.

come on in my kitchen

come on in my kitchen

i'll show you
what flavors
you've been missing
from the illusions of
a land far away
to the very essence
of kissing.

i'll let you stir
the boiling pot
while i taste
your hand holding the brew
and lick the dripping
coffee, off your
espresso lips

even before you have a clue.

coffee maker

she wore a real smile in her eyes
and her face was frosted with brown sugar
and she put the lipstick on
painting a bar-room queen
before the mirror
and her hands were young
and she had a playful ass.
she wore black panties and I got them off
grabbed her breasts and with
coffee brewing in the kitchen
I took her standing up.

as we struggled around the silverware
the coffee maker took a deep breath
and beeped and I came.

we drank coffee and whiskey for hours
and talked reality and went to bed
to sleep it all off.

she took the coffee maker in the morning.

you are not art

You don't have blue skies
in your mind.

You don't have shiny stars
in your eyes.

Your skin isn't golden fire
burning brighter than the Sun.

Your tears don't resemble
raindrops patiently trickling
down my window pane
on a gray rainy day.

Your hair doesn't breathe
flawlessly in the wind.

You don't look like sunrise
when you wake up.

Your voice isn't a tricky
musical arrangement or a
beautiful symphony.

You're not sad or beautiful
enough to become poetry.

You're not broken enough that
artists would die to paint your
scars on their canvas with

every color they could find
until they lost you in the
setting sun.

You are not art.

You are just plain and dull.

To all of them.

Not to me.

You are not plain and dull.

You are what art
aspires to be.

You are tragically

beautiful.

just maybe

I like the idea
of sipping in
your scents
of amber and

lime while
I suck the orange bitters
of your uncontrolled
desires

escaping your grip
down your lip
and hide you away
in my secret recipe

and turn your secrets
into

a private delicacy.

THREE MORE DAYS

Sundays

it was a Sunday night
and the moon was closing in
like a goodnight kiss,
so quickly that it left
the stars behind
and in the sky
that night
was dusk and
moonlight.

and as i took her hand
in mine
i felt a familiar tune
in my breath
the one that usually
leaves me breathless
time and time again
leaving me satisfied
as my desires loomed
like a flower
moving towards its bloom.

and it didn't take long
for me to transcend into
the nothingness of moonlight
the reflected rays
guiding my sight
to the place i've been before,
a space with
no good or bad

no right or wrong
all acceptance gone
just the night and
that one song

that familiar tune
which made me swoon
that Sunday night

it was more than special
it was, just

right.

THREE MORE DAYS

brave

there are only few things
better than

that song musing your ears again
to belt it
out, in the middle of
the urban bay
while smiling in everyone's eyes
painting over blues and the gray.

but only until the bitter taste
of a bluesy southwest wind
hits you in the face
and the stars draw closer
to your heart than ever.
a strange, sudden urge of
retrospection
that made up the song.

your song.

our song.

and giving in to the bay,
to your heart, and to yourself.

take a deep breath.
in. out. in. outttt.

breathe out.

just look straight ahead
and keep walking.

just please keep walking.

THREE MORE DAYS

after i'm done

i want to

create
write
raw words, and unorthodox
sentences.
weird, but honest
literature.

and to be able to
look myself
in the eyes
after i've done it.

after i'm done
writing about myself.

railroad blues

what's the railroad to me?
you ask.

i never go to see
where it ends
where it takes all those
wanderers

on what corner
it bends.

from all i know
and from what they
say, you'll find out
as you walk
along the way.

it's not the end
but right now, the wind
that's blowing,
i love it enough
to bear

with the not knowing.

THREE MORE DAYS

he's leaving home

saturday morning
at 5 AM
he leaves his clothes
across the hallway
silently closing the door behind
he picks up his keys
and now he's free.

goodbyes are
just some words on a note
that he hoped would say more
and as his friend
tries to recollect her clothes
from the night before
she picks up the note
and clutches her hopes

"love is an adventure
when adventure is love", it said
"i do love you but
if i don't live now
i'd rather be dead."

hollow

she fucked
in a way
that reminded me

less

of homesick nickels
rolling down
the peeling coffee can

and more

of the silence that
follows.

THREE MORE DAYS

end + begin

let's talk about love, she said
her eyes waiting for me
how would you describe it
instead of just letting it be

all of this we talk about
it's just going to be a memory
it did take a long time to find
but something's dead in me
we had laughed, we had played
we had leaned on and let in
and then the leaves turned cold
time always at the end, begins.

as the light drained back to
the window it flooded from
we sat in a dark silence

all things love

gone.

it ain't me

as far as you wish
move away from the light
there's nothing breathing here
go melt in the night
and maybe someone will help you
repay the life you've loaned
whisper you a snowflake
whenever you mourn
someone who gathers flowers all along
from the time you felt reborn

but it ain't me babe
of that i'm sure
don't mistake Lucifer

for the lord.

i drank poetry today

i drank poetry today.

the dripping speck of its black ink
invited my enticing taste buds
to grab a sip from the
hot, steamy brew of words
dreaming together
in the arctic bay breeze.

i brought it closer
to the horizon of my eyes
and wished upon myself
the fortunes of no bias
and lies, even though
the truth was as bitter
as her sly smile,
it was still the truth
in every word, and line.

i drank poetry today.

or maybe
it was just

coffee.

if i die tomorrow

if i die tomorrow
would you
miss me?

would you miss
the dance of naked footsteps
on the cold wooden floor?

would you miss
my voice
in your ears?

would you miss
drowning
in the pool of my coffee eyes?

would you miss
my laugh
echoing through your heart?

would you miss
the way
the rise and the fall
of my chest quickens
when you're near?

would you miss
how I tug at your
heart strings
with such ease?

THREE MORE DAYS

or how easily
you tug at mine?

would you miss
the taste of spices on my skin
from turning my empty house
into a home
whenever I cooked for you?

would there be an empty space
in your heart
from all the times I rested
my ear against you
to listen to it?

your heart.

where you keep a special
place for me.

what about your mind?

will it be sane
when I'm gone?

or
will you always remember
the nights when we dreamed
of having skinny feet
together?

will you remember that

your eyes
are my favorite color?

your hello
is my favorite sound?

your warmth
is my favorite feeling?

will you miss me
the way
I already miss you?

THREE MORE DAYS

love

the love that
made you
was as simple
as

the sounds at dinner:

clinks of pan
on stove.
scraping back of chairs.
hummed melodies.

and intimate dialogues.

coffee and rain

the smell of coffee and rain
takes me back
it's all white and black
to the times
simpler, and sane.

i'll be the last one leavin'
before you close the door
and can't say no more,
i'll lick your inside
slowly sippin'

like my hot black coffee
on a gray, rainy evenin'.

THREE MORE DAYS

smile

i met them two
women, on 4th and Brannan.

their faces had given up
on wrinkles.
their hair was as warm as
the Lord's blessing
any given Sunday.
and colored bright as
Lucifer's face.
their bent backs
pointed towards the future.

one of them had colored
dotted socks on.
maybe they matched.
or was that her trick?
the other one had the
sleight of the bluest southern skies
in her warm blue eyes.

they were both out
and about at an A.M. in the morning
when you'd still be regretting
the existence of your loneliness
or the awkwardness of last night
in your dreams.

them?

I've never seen a smile so contagious.

imagination

her
beauty and
her wild

were way
beyond

her

imagination.

discovery

romance is

a man flirting with the stars
and their glittering home
when he didn't know
about the great depths
of the sea.

it was wanting
to discover you,
to reveal the best
of those hidden gems
inside you

when i still
hadn't found

me.

a new language

how am i supposed to write words down?

when words no longer feel real
when everything this heart says
feels like a trick
of those apathetic words.

breathing is my new language.
one that has always been
unacknowledged.

the translation.
the pitch.
the heave.
the thrill.
the profoundness.

it has it all.

moans like a saxophone
joyful, like trumpets
rhymes, like jazz.

i play the tune
across your body.
each spot i touch
hits a new note.

creating new vocabulary.

THREE MORE DAYS

the lemon poem

her hands clutched the sheets
desperate for the past
but her mouth had already
spoken of her future

"shake me 'til the juice runs
down my leg"

and she started losing
her space and time
one inch at a moment
deep inside
her eyes ready to ask
what didn't seem important
enough
and then they held together
that moment for a brief
second and let it all go.

we sighed together and I
remained within her.

her mouth was loosened
surrendered to everything
and then it finally asked
"so what does this mean for us?"

love, let it stay
what is and what should never be.

my foolish heart

i wake up each day
with a promise
in my foolish heart,
for some love
from the days of past,
but this promise
never seems to last
for long.
and just like
the days before
this day is gone,
but with a little hope
for tomorrow
my light shines
out in the blue,
and i fall terribly easily
yet again
for you.

THREE MORE DAYS

we don't have to take our clothes off

take my hand
and lead me to
the floor.

let's hold each other
and move along
as the rhythm goes,
as the music like
the southwesterly breeze
flows.

we can sway
our feet
while your hazel eyes
sing the song
of this cold snap night.

let's just have
fun,
we don't have to take
our clothes off

tonight.

dazed and confused

cold shivered deep in my bones
you also got a hang of it;
your ears are red.

I always thought of how the chill
that numbed my face
was a different temperature to us;

you felt winter in the dawn
of spring.

lately you've been sharing it
without thrusting the knife
through the solitude of rain

warming up your core.

your reflection in the puddles
is as distorted as
your way of thinking.

three more days

hold my hand
and walk with me
i'll show you the mountains
of my emptiness
i'll slip you into
the canyons of my loneliness

close your eyes
and listen to me
i'll play you the dark
coming down tonight
i'll kiss you the stars
hidden in its silent lies

we'll walk us together
and pass this through our lives
give it three more days babe
and you'll be gone from mine

open the letter
and read it all
i've written you phrases
that dreamers dream
i've doodled you a canvas
a masterpiece it seems

wipe those tears
and rip it all
i've done you wrong
and kept you apart
go, walk straight and
haunt my heart

we'll dust us off together
and pass this through our lives
give it three more days babe
and we'll be gone from mine.

THREE MORE DAYS

THREE MORE DAYS

CONCLUSION

"You just need to sit down and write it."

I can't. Not everyone can just sit down, open a vein and start bleeding.

She grabs my hair and pulls my head back until I can read a pair of hazel eyes. There is something about those eyes that I always struggle with while translating their existence into words.

"Just do it already, you're pathetic."

She wouldn't stop talking. Her voice always aiming for the back of my head. Today those hazel eyes are just that, a pair of eyes. Anything, but inspiration.

I try to pull my hair from her grip, but it's too firm.

"If we're waiting for your inspiration to arrive we could be here the rest of the year." She yanks my head to one side and let go of me.

I listen to my own breathing while my hands find solace in my hair. I finally grab a chair and thought about it.

Why is this so hard? Why couldn't I bring myself to do this?

I'm such a failure.

"Glad we at least agree on that."

She sighs, while leaning on the desk across from me and sipping my wine with her espresso lips. I can see her clearly now. The dark under her eyes brings out her shrilling green eyes. And inside those eyes is my reflection looking back at me through a new perspective.

I wish I could just shut her out. Her voice is like knives cutting through my skull. Every syllable she utters feels like a year without love.

Love.

"For fuck's sake, don't get sentimental now, you know you did that to yourself."

A ray of light, born some thousand years ago, pierces through the smoke and lights up my dark room. Soon the sun is going to rise. Another night gone, another night wasted.

A thought flows through my head like it has done so many times before. I try to capture it before it flies by my hand. But this time I did it. I don't know how long it took me, but looking out the window, I can see the first rays peeking through the holes.

"You're weak."

I know.

The seed that was planted only needs those first rays. It starts to sprout, and vines and flowers starts shooting up in the air one by one. For the first time in my distant memory, it looks pretty from where I'm standing.

Breathtaking.

THREE MORE DAYS

I stand up swiftly. The gentle cry of my chair hitting the floor echoes through my mind.

"You finally realized you're never going to succeed at this?"

I look up and notice her staring at me. Her deep blue eyes have lost all the jazz that was once there.

My glass is empty by now. I take the bottle of wine and walk over to the window. I bring the bottle to my lips while looking over the city slowly waking up.

"Can't we go back?"

I hate the begging that can be heard clearly in my voice.

No answer.

I take another sip.

Still nothing.

I turn around slowly and face an empty room.

I'm just now realizing that no one was ever here.

ABOUT THE AUTHOR

If you've read the book, you already know.

www.ingramcontent.com/pod-product-compliance
Lightning Source LLC
Chambersburg PA
CBHW061343040426
42444CB00011B/3059